This Fishing Journal

BELONGS TO

_____

_____

Eat. Sleep. Fish.

DATE:

LOCATION:

WEATHER:

BAIT USED

FISH CAUGHT	WEIGHT

Notes About My Trip

Eat. Sleep. Fish.

DATE:

LOCATION:

WEATHER:

BAIT USED

FISH CAUGHT	WEIGHT

Notes About My Trip

Eat. Sleep. Fish.

DATE:

LOCATION:

WEATHER:

BAIT USED

FISH CAUGHT	WEIGHT

Notes About My Trip

Eat. Sleep. Fish.

DATE:

LOCATION:

WEATHER:

BAIT USED

FISH CAUGHT	WEIGHT

Notes About My Trip

Eat. Sleep. Fish.

DATE:

LOCATION:

WEATHER:

BAIT USED

FISH CAUGHT	WEIGHT

Notes About My Trip

_____

_____

_____

_____

_____

_____

_____

_____

_____

_____

_____

_____

_____

_____

Eat. Sleep. Fish.

DATE: _____

LOCATION: _____

WEATHER: _____

BAIT USED

FISH CAUGHT	WEIGHT

Notes About My Trip

Eat. Sleep. Fish.

DATE:

LOCATION:

WEATHER:

BAIT USED

FISH CAUGHT	WEIGHT

Notes About My Trip

Eat. Sleep. Fish.

DATE:

LOCATION:

WEATHER:

BAIT USED

FISH CAUGHT	WEIGHT

Notes About My Trip

_____

_____

_____

_____

_____

_____

_____

_____

_____

_____

_____

_____

_____

_____

_____

Eat. Sleep. Fish.

DATE:

LOCATION:

WEATHER:

BAIT USED

FISH CAUGHT	WEIGHT

Notes About My Trip

_____

_____

_____

_____

_____

_____

_____

_____

_____

_____

_____

_____

_____

_____

Eat. Sleep. Fish.

DATE:

LOCATION:

WEATHER:

BAIT USED

FISH CAUGHT	WEIGHT

Notes About My Trip

_____

_____

_____

_____

_____

_____

_____

_____

_____

_____

_____

_____

_____

_____

Eat. Sleep. Fish.

DATE:

LOCATION:

WEATHER:

BAIT USED

FISH CAUGHT	WEIGHT

Notes About My Trip

_____

_____

_____

_____

_____

_____

_____

_____

_____

_____

_____

_____

_____

_____

_____

Eat. Sleep. Fish.

DATE:

LOCATION:

WEATHER:

BAIT USED

FISH CAUGHT	WEIGHT

Notes About My Trip

Eat. Sleep. Fish.

DATE:

LOCATION:

WEATHER:

BAIT USED

FISH CAUGHT	WEIGHT

Notes About My Trip

_____

_____

_____

_____

_____

_____

_____

_____

_____

_____

_____

_____

_____

Eat. Sleep. Fish.

DATE: _____

LOCATION: _____

WEATHER: _____

BAIT USED

FISH CAUGHT	WEIGHT

Notes About My Trip

_____

_____

_____

_____

_____

_____

_____

_____

_____

_____

_____

_____

Eat. Sleep. Fish.

DATE:

LOCATION:

WEATHER:

BAIT USED

FISH CAUGHT	WEIGHT

Notes About My Trip

_____

_____

_____

_____

_____

_____

_____

_____

_____

_____

_____

_____

_____

_____

Eat. Sleep. Fish.

DATE:

LOCATION:

WEATHER:

BAIT USED

FISH CAUGHT	WEIGHT

Notes About My Trip

_____

_____

_____

_____

_____

_____

_____

_____

_____

_____

_____

_____

_____

_____

_____

Eat. Sleep. Fish.

DATE:

LOCATION:

WEATHER:

BAIT USED

FISH CAUGHT	WEIGHT

Notes About
My Trip

Eat. Sleep. Fish.

DATE:

LOCATION:

WEATHER:

BAIT USED

FISH CAUGHT	WEIGHT

Notes About My Trip

Eat. Sleep. Fish.

DATE:

LOCATION:

WEATHER:

BAIT USED

FISH CAUGHT	WEIGHT

Notes About My Trip

_____

_____

_____

_____

_____

_____

_____

_____

_____

_____

_____

_____

_____

Eat. Sleep. Fish.

DATE:

LOCATION:

WEATHER:

BAIT USED

FISH CAUGHT	WEIGHT

Notes About My Trip

Eat. Sleep. Fish.

DATE: _____

LOCATION: _____

WEATHER: _____

BAIT USED

FISH CAUGHT	WEIGHT

Notes About My Trip

_____

_____

_____

_____

_____

_____

_____

_____

_____

_____

_____

_____

_____

Eat. Sleep. Fish.

DATE:

LOCATION:

WEATHER:

BAIT USED

FISH CAUGHT	WEIGHT

Notes About
My Trip

_____

_____

_____

_____

_____

_____

_____

_____

_____

_____

_____

_____

_____

Eat. Sleep. Fish.

DATE: _____

LOCATION: _____

WEATHER: _____

BAIT USED

FISH CAUGHT	WEIGHT

Notes About My Trip

Eat. Sleep. Fish.

DATE: |_____|

LOCATION: |_____|

WEATHER: |_____|

BAIT USED

FISH CAUGHT	WEIGHT

Notes About
My Trip

_____

_____

_____

_____

_____

_____

_____

_____

_____

_____

_____

_____

Eat. Sleep. Fish.

DATE:

LOCATION:

WEATHER:

BAIT USED

FISH CAUGHT	WEIGHT

Notes About My Trip

Eat. Sleep. Fish.

DATE:

LOCATION:

WEATHER:

BAIT USED

FISH CAUGHT	WEIGHT

Notes About My Trip

Eat. Sleep. Fish.

DATE: [   ]

LOCATION: [   ]

WEATHER: [   ]

BAIT USED

FISH CAUGHT	WEIGHT

Notes About
My Trip

_____

_____

_____

_____

_____

_____

_____

_____

_____

_____

_____

_____

_____

_____

Eat. Sleep. Fish.

DATE:

LOCATION:

WEATHER:

BAIT USED

FISH CAUGHT	WEIGHT

Notes About My Trip

Eat. Sleep. Fish.

DATE:

LOCATION:

WEATHER:

BAIT USED

FISH CAUGHT	WEIGHT

Notes About My Trip

_____

_____

_____

_____

_____

_____

_____

_____

_____

_____

_____

_____

_____

_____

Eat. Sleep. Fish.

DATE: _____

LOCATION: _____

WEATHER: _____

BAIT USED

FISH CAUGHT	WEIGHT

Notes About My Trip

Eat. Sleep. Fish.

DATE:

LOCATION:

WEATHER:

BAIT USED

FISH CAUGHT	WEIGHT

Notes About My Trip

_____

_____

_____

_____

_____

_____

_____

_____

_____

_____

_____

_____

_____

_____

Eat. Sleep. Fish.

DATE:

LOCATION:

WEATHER:

BAIT USED

FISH CAUGHT	WEIGHT

Notes About My Trip

_____

_____

_____

_____

_____

_____

_____

_____

_____

_____

_____

_____

_____

Eat. Sleep. Fish.

DATE:

LOCATION:

WEATHER:

BAIT USED

FISH CAUGHT	WEIGHT

Notes About
My Trip

_____

_____

_____

_____

_____

_____

_____

_____

_____

_____

_____

_____

_____

_____

Eat. Sleep. Fish.

DATE:

LOCATION:

WEATHER:

BAIT USED

FISH CAUGHT	WEIGHT

Notes About
My Trip

Eat. Sleep. Fish.

DATE:

LOCATION:

WEATHER:

BAIT USED

FISH CAUGHT	WEIGHT

Notes About My Trip

Eat. Sleep. Fish.

DATE:

LOCATION:

WEATHER:

BAIT USED

FISH CAUGHT	WEIGHT

Notes About My Trip

_____

_____

_____

_____

_____

_____

_____

_____

_____

_____

_____

_____

_____

_____

Eat. Sleep. Fish.

DATE:

LOCATION:

WEATHER:

BAIT USED

FISH CAUGHT	WEIGHT

Notes About
My Trip

Eat. Sleep. Fish.

DATE: _____

LOCATION: _____

WEATHER: _____

BAIT USED

FISH CAUGHT	WEIGHT

Notes About
My Trip

_____

_____

_____

_____

_____

_____

_____

_____

_____

_____

_____

_____

_____

_____

_____

_____

Eat. Sleep. Fish.

DATE:

LOCATION:

WEATHER:

BAIT USED

FISH CAUGHT	WEIGHT

Notes About My Trip

_____

_____

_____

_____

_____

_____

_____

_____

_____

_____

_____

_____

_____

_____

_____

Eat. Sleep. Fish.

DATE:

LOCATION:

WEATHER:

BAIT USED

FISH CAUGHT	WEIGHT

Notes About My Trip

_____

_____

_____

_____

_____

_____

_____

_____

_____

_____

_____

_____

_____

_____

_____

Eat. Sleep. Fish.

DATE:

LOCATION:

WEATHER:

BAIT USED

FISH CAUGHT	WEIGHT

Notes About My Trip

_____

_____

_____

_____

_____

_____

_____

_____

_____

_____

_____

_____

_____

_____

_____

Eat. Sleep. Fish.

DATE:

LOCATION:

WEATHER:

BAIT USED

FISH CAUGHT	WEIGHT

Notes About
My Trip

_____

_____

_____

_____

_____

_____

_____

_____

_____

_____

_____

_____

_____

_____

_____

_____

Eat. Sleep. Fish.

DATE:

LOCATION:

WEATHER:

BAIT USED

FISH CAUGHT	WEIGHT

Notes About
My Trip

_____

_____

_____

_____

_____

_____

_____

_____

_____

_____

_____

_____

_____

_____

_____

Eat. Sleep. Fish.

DATE: _____

LOCATION: _____

WEATHER: _____

BAIT USED

FISH CAUGHT	WEIGHT

Notes About My Trip

_____

_____

_____

_____

_____

_____

_____

_____

_____

_____

_____

_____

_____

_____

_____

Eat. Sleep. Fish.

DATE:

LOCATION:

WEATHER:

BAIT USED

FISH CAUGHT	WEIGHT

Notes About My Trip

_____

_____

_____

_____

_____

_____

_____

_____

_____

_____

_____

_____

_____

_____

_____

_____

Eat. Sleep. Fish.

DATE:

LOCATION:

WEATHER:

BAIT USED

FISH CAUGHT	WEIGHT

Notes About My Trip

_____

_____

_____

_____

_____

_____

_____

_____

_____

_____

_____

_____

_____

_____

_____

Eat. Sleep. Fish.

DATE:

LOCATION:

WEATHER:

BAIT USED

FISH CAUGHT	WEIGHT

Notes About My Trip

Eat. Sleep. Fish.

DATE:

LOCATION:

WEATHER:

BAIT USED

FISH CAUGHT	WEIGHT

Notes About
My Trip

Eat. Sleep. Fish.

DATE:

LOCATION:

WEATHER:

BAIT USED

FISH CAUGHT	WEIGHT

Notes About My Trip

Eat. Sleep. Fish.

DATE:

LOCATION:

WEATHER:

BAIT USED

FISH CAUGHT	WEIGHT

Notes About My Trip

_____

_____

_____

_____

_____

_____

_____

_____

_____

_____

_____

_____

_____

_____

Eat. Sleep. Fish.

DATE:

LOCATION:

WEATHER:

BAIT USED

FISH CAUGHT	WEIGHT

Notes About
My Trip

_____

_____

_____

_____

_____

_____

_____

_____

_____

_____

_____

_____

_____

Made in the USA
Lexington, KY
01 June 2019